## AND GOD CREATED SCIENCE

# EXPLORING WEATHER

**30 AMAZING PROJECTS THAT TEACH THE WONDERS OF GOD'S CREATION**

## STEPHANIE FINKE

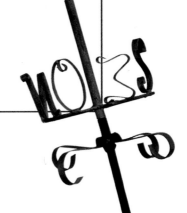

PROMISE
PRESS

An Imprint of Barbour Publishing

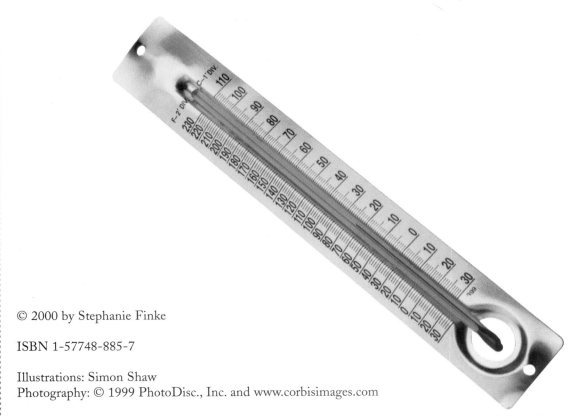

© 2000 by Stephanie Finke

ISBN 1-57748-885-7

Illustrations: Simon Shaw
Photography: © 1999 PhotoDisc., Inc. and www.corbisimages.com

Published by Promise Press, an imprint of Barbour Publishing, Inc., P.O. Box 719, Uhrichsville, Ohio 44683
http://www.barbourbooks.com

 Member of the
Evangelical Christian
Publishers Association

Printed in the United States of America.

# TABLE OF CONTENTS

# RAIN TO RAINBOWS

*"God's voice thunders in marvelous ways;*
*he does great things beyond our understanding.*
*He says to the snow, 'fall on the earth,'*
*and to the rain shower, 'be a mighty downpour.'"*
*Job 37:5-6*

**People** are preoccupied with the weather. Is it going to rain on the picnic? Will there be snow for sledding? Will there be enough water for the crops to grow? Weather is one of God's creations that affects us every day. It  may be in a small way, such as whether or not to carry an umbrella, or it may be in the heart stopping fury of a thunderstorm.

Watching the weather gives us an incredible opportunity to experience God's creation of nature firsthand. We can catch gently falling snowflakes and look at the intricate patterns or gaze at the untamed beauty of lightning crashing to the ground. No matter where we live on this planet, God's weather affects our lives in very intimate ways.

Dear God,
Thank You for the weather and all it brings, from wind and sun to fog and lightning. Let us appreciate each day with the weather it brings and help us to understand Your amazing creation.
Amen.

# GOD'S GREAT WATER CYCLE

*...if he is thirsty, give him water to drink.*
*Proverbs 25:21*

**Pour** a glass full of water. Look at it closely; clear, pure, and thirst-quenching, water hasn't changed since the very beginning of the earth. Take a sip. You are drinking the same water that God used to fill the ancient seas. The only difference is that your water has been through the water cycle a few million times.

No, it's not like the rinse cycle on the washing machine, but the water cycle does clean water. It works because water alters its form with changes in temperature. Water is in a liquid state when it is between 32 degrees Fahrenheit (0 degrees Celsius) and 211 degrees Fahrenheit (99 degrees Celsius). When the temperature drops below 32 degrees Fahrenheit, water becomes the solid known as ice. At temperatures above 211 degrees Fahrenheit, water changes into a gas and can be seen as steam.

What You Need:
- Empty 2-liter clear plastic pop bottle and lid
- Pointed scissors
- Potting soil
- Seeds
- Boiling hot water
- Adult assistance

The heat of the sun shining on large bodies of water, such as oceans and lakes, causes water to change into a gas. This process is called evaporation. As the gas moves into the air, it collects together to form clouds.

When a great deal of water is held in the clouds, they reach the saturation point and liquid water is released back to the ground. This is called precipitation and can come in the form of rain, snow, sleet, or even a solid called hail.

When the precipitation reaches the ground, the whole cycle starts over again. No new water is made. The same water is simply used over and over again in God's great water cycle.

You can make your own miniature water cycle.

Thoroughly rinse the empty bottle in warm water and remove any labels.

Use the scissors to cut the bottle in two, leaving a 3-inch rim on the base of the bottle. Set the bottom segments aside (see illustration A).

Stand the top of the bottle in the pan of boiling tap water for one minute. Have an adult help with this part. This will shrink the top slightly and allow it to slide easily into the base (see illustration B).

Take the base of the bottle you have set aside and fill the bottom with potting soil. Plant your seeds in the soil and water it until the soil is damp but not overflowing.

Insert the top of the bottle into the base to enclose the terrarium. Use clear tape around the edge where the bottle was cut to make a watertight seal (see illustration C).

Place the water cycle in a warm, sunny window. Within a day or two, the water will condense at the top of the bottle, and it will begin to "rain." In two weeks you should begin to see the seeds sprout and grow as the "rain" falls. This mini water cycle will continue to work for years. God's water cycle will last until eternity.

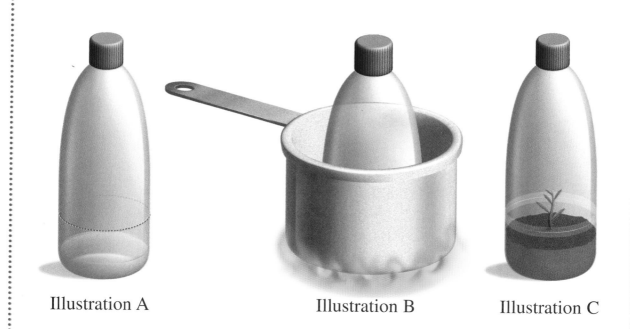

Illustration A       Illustration B       Illustration C

# AIR IS THERE

*God saw all that he had made,*
*and it was very good.*
*And there was evening,*
*and there was morning—the sixth day.*
*Thus the heavens and the earth were*
*completed in all their vast array.*
*Genesis 1:31, 2:1*

**Take** a deep breath and hold it. Put your hand in front of your face and let out your breath. You just felt moving air. Air is the mixture of gases that covers the surface of the earth like a protective blanket. The mixture acts as an insulator deflecting harmful rays from the sun and keeping heat on the earth during the night. God's amazing gift of air is called the atmosphere.

The atmosphere is essential to life on Earth. It contains both the oxygen that animals breathe and the carbon dioxide plants need for photosynthesis. Stretching 600 miles above the surface of the planet, the atmosphere is divided into four layers: the troposphere, stratosphere, mesosphere, and thermosphere.

The first layer, called the troposphere, is only 6 to 10 miles high, but it contains all the air we breathe and all the weather that effects the earth. The upper layers of air are usually calm and unchanging. The air there holds little water and has no weather. These are the layers of insulation that help absorb the rays of the sun. The outer layer of atmosphere, the thermosphere, can reach a blistering 3,600 degrees Fahrenheit (2,000 degrees Celsius). Imagine what would happen to the earth without God's protective blanket of atmosphere.

What You Need:

• Tall drinking glass
• Sink full of water
• Facial tissue or paper towel

Try this experiment to see how God protects the earth with a layer of air.

Stuff the paper into the bottom of the glass. Make sure there is at least a 2- to 3-inch space between the paper and the mouth of the glass. Turn the glass so the open end is facing down toward the water in the sink. Make sure you are holding the glass perfectly level.

Push the glass into the sink full of water. Do not tilt the glass. Keep it level as you push it down to the bottom. Then slowly pull the glass out.

Feel the paper inside the glass. It is not wet! That is because a layer of air was trapped between the water and the paper. That air protected the paper from getting wet, the same way God uses a blanket of air to protect the earth from the heat of the sun.

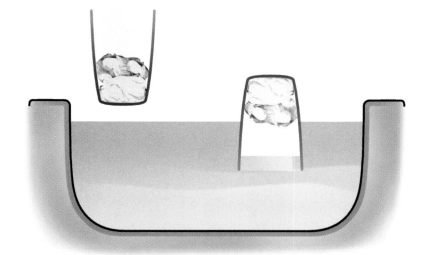

# HEAVY AIR

*The LORD abhors dishonest scales, but accurate weights are his delight.*

*proverbs 11:1*

**Objects** that are small and easy to lift are often referred to as being "lighter than air." This expression implies that air is so light that it has no weight. But scientists have been able to measure the weight of the molecules that make up air, and they estimate that the total weight of the air surrounding the earth is about 5.75 quadrillion tons. Not even Samson himself could lift that much air.

You can learn that air has weight with this experiment.

Blow up the balloons until they are the same size and tie them off. Gently place a small piece of masking tape on the side of one balloon. Tie a small circle of string to the end of each balloon. (Make sure each piece of string is the same size.)

Bend the paperclips to form two hooks and hang them on opposite ends of the coat hanger. Hold the pencil level in the air and have your friend place the hook of the coat hanger on the pencil. Make sure the paperclip

## What You Need:

- Wire coat hanger
- Two balloons of equal size
- Two paperclips
- String
- Masking tape
- Needle
- Pencil
- A friend or assistant

hooks are at opposite sides of the coat hanger. Put one balloon on each hook. The coat hanger should be balanced, because the weight of each balloon is equal.

Have your friend use the needle to carefully poke a hole through the masking tape on one balloon. Let the air slowly escape from the balloon and observe the coat hanger. The balloon that is full of air weighs more than the balloon that is empty.

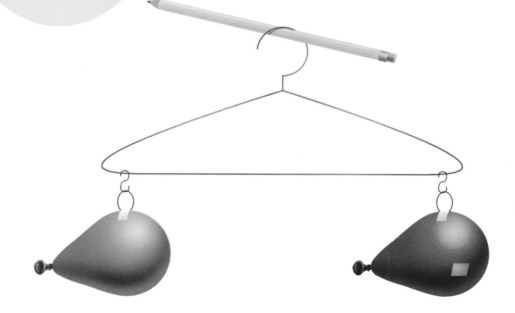

# UNDER PRESSURE

*The birds of the air nest by the waters.*

*Psalm 104:12*

**Air** constantly surrounds us. We walk through air, breathe air into our lungs, and use it to inflate balloons. Our bodies are so used to the presence of air that we don't even notice its weight.

Air weighs 14.7 pounds per square inch. That means that the weight of the air pressing down on your body is nearly one ton (2,240 pounds or 1,016.05 kilograms).

You say it doesn't feel like there's a ton of air resting on your shoulders? That's because the pressure of the air pressing from the outside is equal to the amount of air that is inside your body. Place your hands together in front of your chest and push. Neither hand moves. That is because the pressure is equal.

When the air pressure outside your body changes, you can feel it when you ride in an elevator or fly in an airplane.

You can witness the strength of air pressure with this experiment.

Fill the cup with water all the way to the brim. Place the tagboard over the top of the cup. Use your palm to press the tagboard firmly to rim of the cup. Use your other hand to turn the cup upside down over the sink. Then remove your hand from the tagboard.

The water will stay in the cup! This is because the air pressure pushing up on the tagboard is greater than the pressure of the water pushing down.

What You Need:
- Cup
- Square piece of tagboard, 4 inches by 4 inches
- Water
- Sink or tub

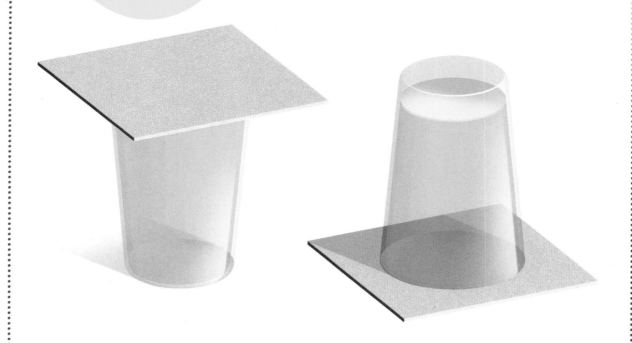

# SLIGHTLY SLANTED

*And God said, "Let there be lights
in the expanse of the sky
to separate the day from the night,
and let them serve as signs to mark seasons and
days and years."*
*Genesis 1:14*

**Seasons** are a part of
God's design for the earth.
With the change in seasons
come many changes in the
weather. Some parts of the
world have four distinct seasons with a cold winter that
includes ice and snow and a
warm summer with little rain
and hot temperatures. Other
parts of the world have just
two seasons, either dry or
rainy.

Two things cause the
changing seasons, the shape
of the earth and the way the
earth spins on its axis. The

What You Need:

- *Adult helper*
- *Desk lamp*
- *Orange*
- *Knitting needle*
- *Thick piece of Styrofoam*
- *Dark room*

earth is a sphere-shaped (round) planet. It spins on an imaginary line that runs from the North Pole to the South Pole. This imaginary line is called the axis. The axis of the earth is not exactly vertical. It is slightly slanted with a tilt of 23 degrees.

As the earth orbits around the sun, the North Pole is slanted away from the sun for half the year and toward the sun for the other half. That slanted tilt combined with the shape of the earth causes different places on the planet to receive different amounts of sunlight.

To better understand the way God made the seasons, try these simple experiments.

Have an adult push the knitting needle through the orange. The needle represents the earth's axis, and the orange is the earth. Stick the needle in the Styrofoam base so that the needle is slanted 23 degrees. This is the tilt of the earth as it orbits the sun.

Place the orange in front of the desk lamp with the needle pointed toward the lamp. This represents the earth during the summer in Europe and North America. Notice how the sun shines brightly on the North Pole and is dimmer on the South Pole.

The shape of the earth also causes the amount of sunlight to vary from place to place.

Have your friend hold the orange in the dark room. Shine the flashlight directly onto the middle of the orange. The orange is the earth, and the light represents the rays of the sun. Notice how bright the light is at the center of the earth. The earth has an imaginary line called the equator halfway between the North Pole and the South Pole. The sun's light is most intense at the equator because it receives the direct sunlight. Moving away from the equator, the earth receives indirect sunlight, which is not as strong and does not make as much heat.

The uneven heating—due to the planet's shape and tilt—makes the seasons and creates the changes in temperature that cause the weather.

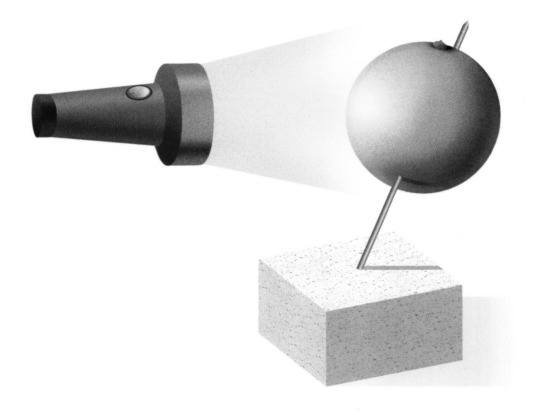

# BLACK HEAT

*It rises at one end
of the heavens
and makes its circuit
to the other;
nothing is hidden
from its heat.*

*Psalm 19:6*

**Even** in King David's time, people struggled with the heat of the sun. They understood that the light of the sun was necessary for their crops to grow, but the intensity of the summer sun was sometimes unbearable.

In today's modern world of thermometers and weather forecasters, meteorologists often warn people about high temperatures by issuing heat warnings. In some parts of the world, the combination of heat and humidity can become dangerous. When people are exposed to extreme temperatures for long periods of time, water evaporates from the pores of their skin and can cause dehydration. Heat exhaustion or heat stroke can occur when a person's body temperature rises from too much sun. If the body gets too warm, it can even result in death.

Drinking plenty of water and staying in the shade are two ways to protect yourself from too much sun. Another way is to wear clothing that reflects the heat. Light colors reflect the light of the sun and keep people and objects cooler, while dark colors absorb the sun's heat and light.

Test the temperature difference between light and dark colors.

Paint one-half of the board black and the other half white. After the paint has dried, place the board in an area where it will receive sun for at least an hour. Place one thermometer on the black half of the board and the other thermometer on the white half of the board. Use your pencil and paper to record the temperatures. Check the thermometers every fifteen minutes and record any temperature changes.

Your experiment should prove that it is better to wear a white T-shirt on a summer day. Would a black or white coat be better for winter?

What You Need:
- Sunny area outside
- Two thermometers
- White and black paint
- Paintbrushes
- Two pieces of board or cardboard at least 10 inches by 5 inches
- Pencil and paper

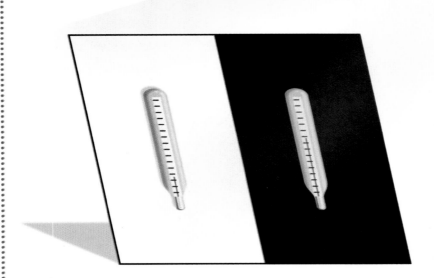

# SUN AND WIND

A furious squall came up, and the waves
broke over the boat,
so that it was nearly swamped.
Jesus was in the stern, sleeping on a cushion.
The disciples woke him and said to him,
"Teacher, don't you care if we drown?"
He got up, rebuked the wind
and said to the waves,
"Quiet! Be still!" Then the wind died down
and it was completely calm.

Mark 4:37-39

**The** story of Jesus calming the wind is such a familiar Bible story that we sometimes forget what an incredible miracle this was. Jesus showed the disciples He was God's Son with His ability to control one of the basic elements of nature, the wind.

Wind is an incredible force. It moves clouds, creates weather patterns, and can cause catastrophic change through tornadoes and hurricanes. All this power begins with some air and little sunshine. Air is a mixture of tiny particles of gases called molecules. The more molecules there are in a given space, the heavier the air.

As air heats up, the molecules begin to move faster and they spread out. The same amount of air holds fewer molecules and thus weighs less. When air is cold, the molecules move slower and stay closer together.

When air is warm, it expands. Cold air contracts. This is the reason that hot air balloons can fly. It is also what makes wind.

When the sun warms the air, it expands and begins to move faster. As it cools off by reaching mountains or cold polar regions, the air contracts and sinks. This causes another movement in the air, or more wind. The heating and cooling of the earth's air goes on every day, and this is what makes wind.

To see the effect of heating and cooling air, try this simple experiment.

Place the balloon over the mouth of the pop bottle. Do not inflate the balloon. The balloon acts as a seal to keep the air trapped inside the bottle. With the help of an adult, use the tongs to place the pop bottle in the pan of boiling water. Hold the bottle in the pan for three or four minutes. What

What You Need:

- Empty 2-liter clear plastic pop bottle without lid
- Pan of boiling water
- One balloon
- Mixing bowl full of ice
- Tongs
- Adult helper

happens to the balloon? Do you see evidence of the air in the balloon expanding?

Remove the bottle from the boiling water and place it directly into the bowl of ice. Leave it in the ice for five minutes. What happens to the balloon? Do you see evidence of the air contracting?

# WHICH WAY THE WIND?

*He makes the clouds his chariot*
*and rides on the wings of the wind.*
*Psalm 104:3*

**Is** it a winter storm coming in from the north or a summer breeze from the south? It all depends on where you live.

When God created the earth, He made the equator region constantly warm and the polar regions constantly cool. This causes the earth to have some basic wind patterns that generally blow in the same direction. These constant wind patterns are called the prevailing winds.

One of the prevailing wind patterns is no wind. The area near the equator receives so much warm sunshine that the hot air rises almost straight up and there is very little wind. This is the area of the equatorial doldrums.

The warm air rising by the equator allows cool air to move in. This constant flow of air above and below the equator is known as the trade winds. The captains of early sailing ships used these winds to help them reach foreign lands.

The horse latitudes are narrow bands of air that are located about 30 degrees north latitude and 30 degrees south latitude. This is air that has warmed near the equator and now cooled. The air sinks straight down and causes a region of very little wind. Early sailors that were caught in these winds were forced to dump cargo from their ships to make them light enough to move in the slow wind. At times, captains even had to dump horses and that is why it is called the horse latitudes.

That warm air that sinks in the horse latitude is pulled toward the colder North Pole and South Pole and produces steady winds that blow from the west to the east. These winds cover almost all of the United States and Europe in the Northern Hemisphere. In the Southern Hemisphere, southern Australia, New Zealand, and the tip of South America benefit from these prevailing westerlies.

The polar easterlies are created when the warm air flows northward to the North Pole and cold air moves southward. The opposite happens at the South Pole. You can study the direction of the wind in

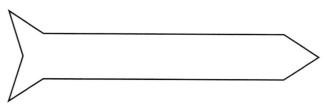

Arrow Pattern

your own part of the world by building a weather vane.

Use the pencil and make a pattern of the arrow on the tracing paper. Cut out the arrow pattern and trace it onto the tagboard. Cut out the tagboard arrow and place the pin through the center. Push the pin holding the arrow into the top of the pencil. Make sure the arrow turns freely on the pin.

Set the pencil and arrow aside and mark the cardboard box with the pen with the correct directions of north, south, east, and west. Use the mat knife to cut a small hole in the center of the bottom of the box. Make sure the hole is large enough for the pencil to fit snugly. Put the pencil in the hole on the box. Use the modeling clay to anchor the pencil so it will not move.

Place the box outside, away from the protection of trees and buildings. Orient the box so the directions on the box match true north and south. Wait for a breeze to come and record the direction of the wind in your weather log.

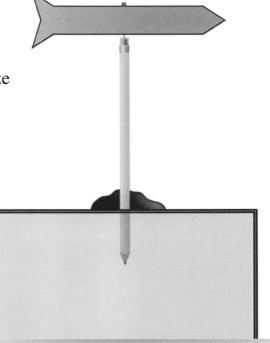

# A QUICK GLANCE

*"The wind blows wherever it pleases.*
*You hear its sound,*
*but you cannot tell where it comes from*
*or where it is going."*

*John 3:8*

The wind is an awesome force in God's world. Made by the expanding and contracting of air, wind can be a gentle spring breeze or it can be an awesome force of destruction flattening buildings and snapping trees with its speed.

The wind not only influences the weather; it also affects the safety of airplanes and ships. In the early 1800s, a British admiral named Francis Beaufort designed a wind scale to help sailors gauge the wind speed at sea. The same scale was adapted for land and allows the average person to accurately judge the speed of the wind.

You can learn to tell the speed of the wind and amaze your friends with your weather knowledge.

Use the Beaufort Wind Scale to watch the wind during the day for one week. Record your observations of how trees and flags move. Use the

Beaufort Wind Scale to predict your wind speed for the day. You may want to record the wind speed two or three different times during the day to see if the speed changes.

In the evening, listen to the radio or watch the local weather report to learn the official wind speed for the day. Compare your observations with the weather report. With practice, you will become an expert at judging the speed of God's wind.

What You Need:
• The Beaufort Wind Scale
• Pencil and paper
• Radio or television

## BEAUFORT WIND SCALE

| Scale # | description | effect on land | MPH |
|---|---|---|---|
| 0 | calm | smoke goes straight up | < 1 |
| 1 | light air | smoke drifts in direction of wind | 1–3 |
| 2 | light breeze | wind felt on face; leaves rustle; flags stir; weather vanes turn | 4–7 |
| 3 | gentle breeze | leaves and twigs move constantly; light flags blow out | 8–12 |
| 4 | moderate breeze | dust, loose papers, and small branches move; flags flap | 13–18 |
| 5 | fresh breeze | small trees in leaf begin to sway; flags ripple | 19–24 |
| 6 | strong breeze | large branches in motion; flags beat; umbrellas turn inside out | 25–31 |
| 7 | moderate gale | whole trees in motion; flags are extended | 32–38 |
| 8 | fresh gale | twigs break off trees; walking is hard | 39–46 |
| 9 | strong gale | slight damage to houses; TV antennas may blow off; awnings rip | 47–54 |
| 10 | whole gale | trees uprooted; much damage to houses | 55–63 |
| 11 | storm | widespread damage | 64–75 |
| 12 | hurricane | excessive damage | > 75 |

# HOW FAST THE WIND?

*He makes the clouds his chariot*
*and rides on the wings of the wind.*
*He makes winds his messengers,*
*flames of fire his servants.*
*Psalm 104:3-4*

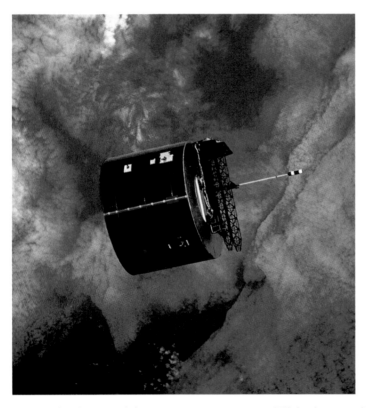

**Understanding** the wind has been important to people throughout the ages. The speed and direction of the wind may be indicators of coming storms. People in biblical times could only watch the sky and movement of the clouds to guess when a storm might be on the horizon. Today scientists use a variety of tools to track the weather—from simple thermometers to radar and satellites.

One tool used to measure wind speed is an anemometer. This invention dates back to 1846 and records the speed of the wind using rotating cups. The wind speed is measured by the number of turns the cups make per minute.

You can measure wind speed by making your own anemometer.

Form a cross with the drinking straws and tape them together at the center. These are the "arms" of your anemometer. These straws will hold the cups.

Have an adult use the scissors to poke a small hole in the side of each drinking cup. The hole should be large enough to push the end of the straw through the cup.

Place one cup on the end of each arm of your straw cross. Make sure all of the cups are facing the same direction. Secure the ends of the straws to the cups with tape.

Push the straight pin through the center of the straw cross. Use the tack hammer to hammer the pin into the top end of the dowel rod. Make sure the straws spin freely on the dowel.

**What You Need:**
- Adult help
- Dowel rod
(½-inch to ¾-inch in diameter)
- Two extra-long drinking straws
- Tape
- Straight pin
- Scissors
- Tack hammer
- Four small drinking cups (3-ounce size)
- Watch with a second hand
- Pencil and paper

You are now ready to take your anemometer outside to check the wind speed. Stick the anemometer in the ground so that the cups can catch the wind. Count the number of complete turns your anemometer makes during one minute. Use your watch to time it. Record the speed with your pencil and paper. Repeat this four more times, then average your totals together. This will be your average wind speed. To see how wind speed changes, do the same experiment every day for a week and record your wind speeds. Does the wind speed stay the same each day? Do windy days bring storms or fair weather? How do your records of wind speed changes compare with local weather forecasts? How can you use the anemometer to learn more about God's incredible force—the wind?

# ANEMOMETER

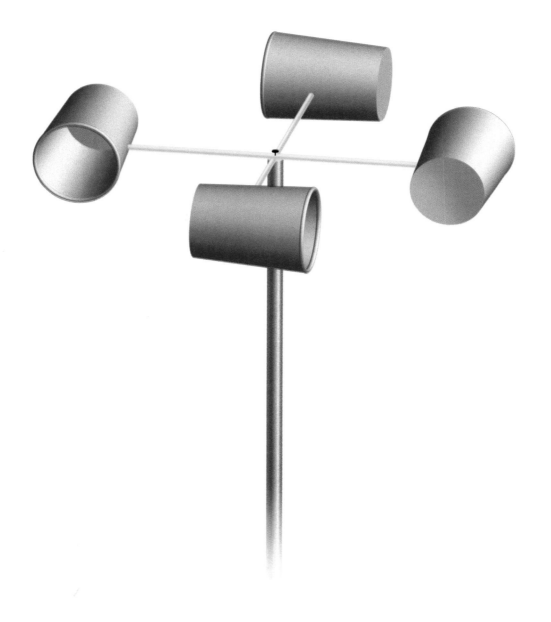

# LAND OR SEA?

*As water disappears from the sea
or a riverbed becomes parched and dry...*
Job 14:11

**Evaporation**—the changing of liquid water to water vapor. It is all a part of God's great water cycle and is necessary to create weather on Earth; yet it can cause humans many problems. Too much evaporation can make sources of fresh water disappear. When evaporation takes place on land without any new rainfall, food crops and other plants will die. Evaporation also takes place over the oceans. But does evaporation occur at the same rate on both land and water?

Many factors determine how fast water evaporates, including the air humidity, amount of sunlight, and temperature. Try this experiment to see which warms up the fastest: soil or water.

Tape the file folders together to form a U-shaped partition. Fill one jar with soil and the other with water. Make sure the water is room temperature. Place the jars at the back of the partition. Tape each of the thermometers to the back of the file folder with the tip of one thermometer in the soil

What You Need:

- Two thermometers
- Flexible desk lamp
- Two glass or plastic jars of equal size
- Soil
- Water
- Two file folders
- Pencil and paper
- Tape

and the tip of the other thermometer in the water. Center the desk lamp over the partition so that each jar is receiving an equal amount of light.

Make a chart and record the temperature for each jar every ten minutes for one hour. You should find that the temperature of the soil increases faster than that of the water.

Land generally tends to heat up faster than bodies of water. This affects the moisture in soil by increasing the rate of evaporation. Any water that is in the soil will quickly turn to water vapor and leave the soil.

Water for plants needs to be continually replenished on the land through rain.

# HIGHS AND LOWS

*Your righteousness reaches to the skies, O God,*
*you who have done great things.*
*Who, O God, is like you?*
*Psalm 71:19*

**God's** creation is absolutely amazing. He created vast mountains, the far reaches of the galaxies, and simple raindrops all from tiny atoms. Atoms are the building blocks of all matter in the universe. Atoms are so tiny that it takes hundreds of them to make up one drop of water, millions of atoms to make a cloud, and trillions of atoms to make up the air that surrounds the earth.

Atoms are not only small, but they are also constantly moving. As the sun heats atoms in the air, they move around more and spread out. This

**What You Need:**

- Stove
- Pan
- Water
- Tub of ice
- Empty 2-liter clear plastic pop bottle and lid

causes the air to become lighter in weight. The warm air expands and rises. Air that cools has atoms that are less active and closer together. This makes the cold air heavier and it sinks. These changes are called changes in air pressure.

You can watch the changes in air pressure at work with this experiment.

*Note: This experiment requires an adult and should only be observed by children.*

Fill the cooking pan with water and let it come to a boil. Take the lid off the empty pop bottle and place the bottom of the bottle in the hot water for two minutes. Remove the bottle from the water and put the lid on the bottle.

Quickly place the entire bottle in the tub of ice. What happens to the bottle?

The atoms of warm air in the bottle contract, and the pressure of the air outside crushes the bottle.

# BUILD A BAROMETER

*He stilled the storm to a whisper;*
*the waves of the sea were hushed.*
*Psalm 107:29*

**One** of the best predictors of changing weather is the air pressure. The weight of the air pushing down on the earth is air pressure. The air pressure changes because of the heating and cooling of the earth. Warm air expands and has less weight, so it does not press down on the earth as much. This is called low pressure, and it usually brings clouds and rain. Air that is cold is much heavier and presses down on the earth harder. This is high pressure and usually brings clear skies and sunshine.

People have been using barometers for many years to measure air pressure. The Italian scientist Torricelli made the first barometer in the 1600s. Since then, barometers have become commonplace, and many people have one in their home.

By watching the changes in barometric pressure, you can learn when the weather will be changing. You can create your own basic barometer to measure air pressure changes.

Fill the bottle to the brim with water. Add some food coloring to the water. Place the bowl on top of the bottle and carefully turn the bottle over so that the bottle is standing up in the bowl.

Lift the bottle very slowly and let some of the water out of the bottle into the bowl until the bottle is about half full.

- Wide-mouth clear bottle
- Plastic bowl
- Masking tape
- Metric ruler
- Water
- Food coloring
- Marking pen
- Scissors
- Construction paper

Cut a strip of construction paper 1 inch wide by 2 inches long. Use the metric ruler and pen to mark the strip with lines every millimeter. Center the strip so that the middle line is even with the level of the water in the bottle.

Tape the strip to the bottle with masking tape. Use the marking pen to highlight where the water level is currently on the paper strip.

Place the barometer on a level spot in the shade. Check the barometer daily.

If the water level rises in the barometer, this means there is high pressure. The heavy air is pushing down on the water in the bowl and causing the water in the barometer to rise. When the air is lightweight, it will not press as hard on the water in the bowl and the water inside the barometer will drop. This is low pressure.

How can watching a barometer help us predict God's ever changing weather?

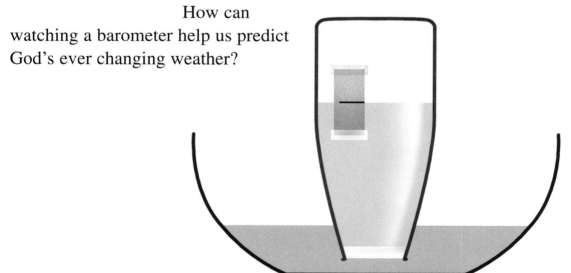

# CREATE A CLOUD

*His favor
is like a rain cloud
in spring.
Proverbs 16:15*

**Take** a bit of dust, some flower pollen, maybe a little soot, mix it all with some water vapor, and what have you got? A cloud, of course! Clouds are created when small particles in the air trap water molecules and hold them in place. When lots of water particles are trapped together, it forms a cloud.

God uses clouds to give moisture to the earth in the form of sleet, snow, and rain. Clouds are an important part of the water cycle. You can create your own cloud inside your house.

Hold the bottle upside down. Have an adult light the birthday candle and hold it inside the mouth of the bottle for seven seconds.

Allow the jug to cool, then

place your mouth over the opening in the bottle and blow air into the container. What happens inside the jug?

You have created a cloud. The candle provided the air particles in the form of soot. The water came from your breath, and together they created a cloud. Next time you gaze at the clouds outside, think what amazing creations God can make with just a little water and some soot.

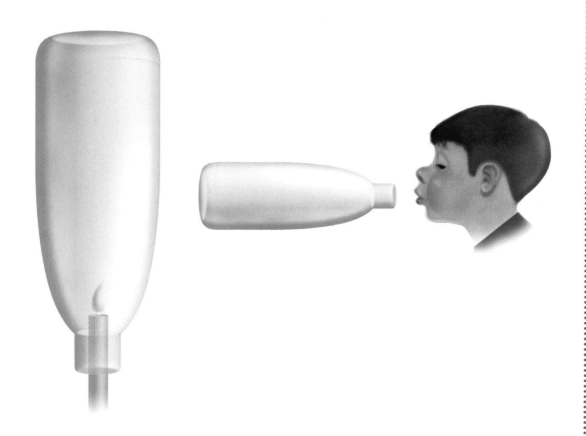

# CLOUD WATCHER

By day the LORD went ahead
of them in a pillar of cloud
to guide them on their way
and by night a pillar of fire
to give them light, so that they could travel by
day or night.
Neither pillar of cloud by day
nor pillar of fire by night
left its place in front of the people.
Exodus 13:21-22

**What You Need:**

- Notebook
- Pencil
- Cloud identification chart
(See page 43)
- Radio or television

**During** the exodus, God used a pillar of cloud to lead the Israelites through the desert, but normally God uses clouds to collect moisture and send us rain.

The clouds we watch floating by are divided into three basic categories. These include the puffy cumulus clouds, the layered stratus clouds, and the feathery cirrus clouds.

Cumulus clouds are large and puffy because they carry the most moisture. As cumulus clouds gather together, they gain more and more water and become cumulonimbus clouds, or rain-bearing clouds.

Cirrus clouds are the light wispy clouds that float high in the sky. These clouds form so high in the atmosphere that they are made of ice crystals. The stratus clouds form in layers as air is forced to rise as it passes over hills.

An important part of predicting the weather is understanding the clouds and the weather they may bring. You can learn more about clouds and how they affect the earth by keeping a cloud log.

Use your notebook to draw and label the clouds you see for a month. Make a daily prediction of what type of weather the clouds will bring. Record the actual weather report for each day to see if your predictions are correct. With a little practice and some keen observation, you will be able to learn how God uses each type of cloud to create the weather.

# CLOUD IDENTIFICATION CHART

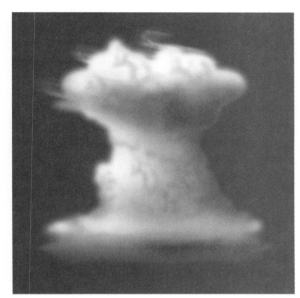

Cumulonimbus

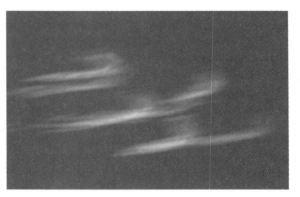

Cirrus

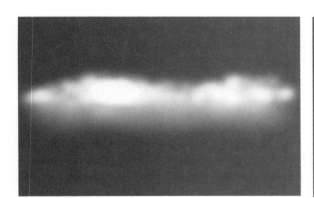

Stratus

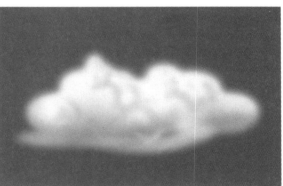

Cumulus

# DEWDROP

*Gideon said to God, "If you will save Israel by my hand as you have promised—look, I will place a wool fleece on the threshing floor. If there is dew only on the fleece and all the ground is dry, then I will know that you will save Israel by my hand, as you said." And that is what happened. Gideon rose early the next day; he squeezed the fleece and wrung out the dew —a bowlful of water.*

*Judges 6:36-40*

**Gideon** used the weather to learn God's will for his life. With the sign of the dew, Gideon knew that God would help him in his battle against Midian. But what is dew, and why was it such a miracle that the fleece (a piece of lamb's wool) was soaked with dew when the grass around it was dry?

Dew is by definition water droplets that form when moisture from the air condenses on the surface of an object. Dew often forms on the grass when the air temperature is warm and the humidity, or the amount of water in the air, is high. Dew can also form on the side of a drinking glass when the glass is full of cold liquid and placed in a warm area.

Conduct this experiment to see why the sign of the dew was a miracle and to learn more about how dew forms.

Place the sponge on the grass. The sponge represents Gideon's fleece. Lay the plastic tarp over the sponge. Leave the tarp on the ground for one to two hours. Return and observe the underside of the tarp. The plastic will be covered with water.

This is dew. It is water that is stored in the ground and in the grass. As the ground warmed up, the water started to evaporate. When the water vapor reached the surface of the plastic, it condensed and created dew. Note that the dew is created evenly over all the tarp. The sponge is also damp from dew. Is there any way you could cause dew to form on the sponge and *not* on the grass?

Gideon had a miraculous weather sign from God!

What You Need:
• Piece of plastic tarp
• grassy area
• Mild spring or summer day
(This experiment won't work in the rain)
• Sponge

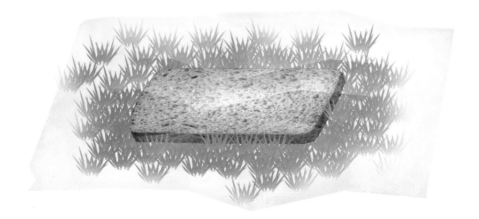

# HOT AND HUMID

*Each man will be like a shelter from the wind
and a refuge from the storm,
like streams of water in the desert...*
*Isaiah 32:2*

**Water** is a precious commodity in the desert. Not only is the desert land dry but so is the air. The desert air holds very little evaporated water. This means it is low in humidity.

Humidity is the amount of water stored in the air. A day that is humid usually feels hot and muggy because there is more water vapor in the air than on an average day.

Meteorologists talk about humidity in terms of percentage of the maximum possible amount of water the air can hold. A cloud has 100 percent humidity while the air over a desert region has a low 10 percent humidity.

When the air is warm, the air molecules are spread farther apart and can hold more water molecules. That is why dew, fog, and mist form in warm climates or warm seasons.

High humidity can also mean a greater chance for rainfall. As the air becomes more and more saturated with water vapor, the liquid water falls from the air to the ground. This is rain.

You can measure the relative humidity by making your own simple hygrometer.

Place both thermometers outside. Place the cotton ball on one thermometer and use the eyedropper to soak the cotton ball with water. Make sure the water is room temperature. Leave the thermometers for five minutes, then record the temperature of each thermometer. Record the temperatures every fifteen minutes for one hour.

If the temperature on the cotton ball thermometer is lower than the other thermometer, there is very little humidity in the air.

The temperature difference would result from evaporation. If the air is dry (not humid), the water will evaporate from the cotton ball. The evaporation will lower the temperature on the thermometer with the cotton ball.

What You Need:

• Two thermometers
• Cotton ball
• Eyedropper full of water

If the air is humid (moist), then there is very little space for new water molecules, and evaporation takes place at a slower rate. Temperatures that are similar on the thermometers indicate high humidity (a high amount of moisture in the air).

# MAKE A MIST

*You are a mist that*
*appears for a little while and then vanishes.*
*James 4:14*

**Mist** and fog are very similar, although the official definition of fog is a low cloud cover that reduces visibility to 600 feet (180 meters) or less. Mist is less dense than fog, but they both form the same way.

Mist and fog are made when water vapor in the air cools and turns back into liquid in the air. They are, in a sense, clouds that form near the surface of the earth. Mist and fog form near the ground overnight because at night the surface of the earth loses its heat. Any water vapor that is in the air near the ground will condense and make a mist.

You can experiment to make your own mist or fog.

Place the crushed ice in the pan. Cover the ice with the salt and stir it all together. Let it stand for three or four minutes. Then lift the pan to your face and gently blow on the mixture. You will see a mist appear.

This mist is made when the water droplets from your breath condense after hitting the surface of the cold ice.

What You Need:
- One cup crushed ice
- Deep pan with a dark lining
- Spoon
- 1/3 cup salt

# MAKE IT RAIN

*"...He causes his sun to rise
on the evil and the good,
and sends rain on the righteous
and the unrighteous."
Matthew 5:45*

**What You Need:**

- Adult helper
- Cooking pot
- Water
- Stove
- Cookie sheet
- Refrigerator
- Pair of oven mitts

**Rain** is a miraculous gift that brings with it life for plants, food for people, and water for all animals to drink. Rain comes to the earth through the evaporation and condensation of the water cycle.

Meteorologists classify rain or precipitation as three different types of events. Drizzle is like a thick fog that falls to the ground. The drops of water from drizzle fall to the ground so slowly that the total precipitation on the ground is too light to measure.

Showers or thundershowers occur in one specific location over a short period of time. Showers happen when a cloud or an area of damp air is suddenly lifted into the atmosphere by the wind. The sudden cooling causes the rain to fall.

The final event is a steady rain. This usually happens when a warm body of air moves over a cold body of air. This causes rain that can last all day or in some parts of the world, several days.

You can make your own rainstorm in your very own kitchen. You will need an adult for this experiment.

Before you begin the experiment, place the cookie sheet in the refrigerator. Fill the cooking pot with water and have an adult bring it to a boil.

Observe the steam that is rising from the pot. This is water vapor, or water that has changed from liquid to gas form.

Once the water is boiling, take the cookie sheet out of the refrigerator. Have an adult put on the oven mitts and hold the cookie sheet over the steam.

Water droplets will form on the cookie sheet, and you will have a mini rain shower over your stove. This occurs because the water vapor condenses, or turns back to liquid (water), as it hits the cold cookie sheet. This is God's water cycle at work.

# RAIN GAUGE

*After a long time, in the third year, the word of the LORD came to Elijah: "Go and present yourself to Ahab, and I will send rain on the land."*

*1 Kings 18:1*

**A drought** is the lack of rain, and it can cause terrible problems for people and animals. A three-year drought, like the one in this Old Testament story, surely caused plants to shrivel and die. Without plants, both animals and people die.

Rain is essential to human survival and, because of this, people are very concerned with how much it rains. Meteorologists keep track of annual (yearly) rainfall all over the world. The average annual rainfall can vary a great deal. Desert regions of the world can receive less than 6 inches of rain per year, while areas of tropical rain forest can receive over 6 feet of rain per year.

The wettest place on the earth is Mount Waialeale, Hawaii. It receives an average of 460 inches (11 meters) of rain each year.

Keeping track of the rainfall in your own backyard can be fun. It is easy to do with a homemade rain gauge.

Place a length of tape vertically on the glass jar. Line the metric ruler up against the tape and use the pen to carefully mark the tape to match the measurements on the ruler. Make sure the ruler has the lowest numbers at the bottom of the jar.

Set the jar on a level place outside, away from trees or overhangs that could cause excess water to drip into the jar.

What You Need:
- *Glass jar with straight sides*
- *Permanent ink pen*
- *Clear plastic tape*
- *Metric ruler*

After it rains, look in the jar and use the measurements to tell how many millimeters of rain fell.

You may want to start a weather log. By recording the amount of rain that falls during each rainstorm, you can compare storm systems and the amount of water each one holds, and you will learn more about God's wonderful water cycle.

# HOW BIG IS A RAINDROP?

*"I will send you rain in its season,*
*and the ground will yield its crops*
*and the trees of the field their fruit."*
Leviticus 26:4

**God's** gift of rain is very important to us. We measure it in buckets and rain gauges and try to predict when it will come. Weather stations all over the world keep records of rainfall averages and record-breaking amounts of rain. People are preoccupied with the rain because it is essential to life here on Earth. Rain is necessary to grow food crops and to fill the lakes and rivers with drinking water. But even with all these statistics, it is very rare to find any information on the size of the average raindrop.

You can measure the size of a raindrop with a simple experiment in your backyard. Cover the bottom of the box lid with flour until the flour is about 2 centimeters deep. Smooth it out with the spatula.

When it begins to rain, place the box lid of flour in the rain. Leave it out until a few drops have made impressions in the flour, then bring it inside. Look closely at the rain pattern. What happens to a raindrop when it hits the ground?

After you have examined the pattern of the raindrops, place the mesh screen on the bowl and pour the flour onto the screen. Do you have any round balls of flour left on the screen? These are preserved raindrops. You can measure the diameter of the drops by placing a ruler next to them. What is the diameter of your largest drop?

What You Need:

• Shallow cardboard box lid
• Flour
• Clean piece of fine mesh screen
• Large mixing bowl
• Large spatula
• Small metric ruler

# WHIRLWIND IN A BOTTLE

*His way is in the whirlwind and the storm.*

*Nahum 1:3*

**The** incredible power of God's weather can be witnessed in the force of a tornado. Tornadoes, or whirlwinds as they are sometimes called, are funnels of spinning air that have enough energy to suck up rocks, trees, and even buildings that are in their paths.

Tornadoes form inside thunderstorm clouds when a column of strongly rising warm air meets the fast-moving upper layers of cold air. The warm air is sent spinning. This whirling column of air forms a vortex, with the air pressure at the center of the tornado much lower than the swirling winds on the outside. Weather instruments that have been sent inside a tornado, and have survived, record wind speeds as high as 280 miles per hour (450 kilometers per hour).

Tornadoes occur on land, and most of the tornadoes in the world occur in the United States of America. The combination of the warm, moist Gulf of Mexico air mixing with cool, dry air moving from the western United States creates perfect conditions for tornado incubation.

Hurricanes also have whirling winds, but they form over water and include torrential rain and are much larger than tornadoes. Hurricanes can be 300 miles (480 kilometers) wide and can last for days. A tornado is no wider than one and one-half miles and only stays on the ground for minutes at a time.

You can create a model of a tornado by making a water vortex.

What You Need:
• Two empty 2-liter clear plastic pop bottles without lids
• Duct tape
• Water
• Food coloring

Fill one bottle three-fourths of the way full with water. Add food coloring to the water and mix it. Center the mouth of the other bottle on top of the bottle that contains the water. Tape the bottles together very tightly with the duct tape.

Leave no gap for water to leak through.

Flip the bottles so that the bottle with the water is on top. Spin the bottles to start the vortex. The water will start spinning, and you have created a model of one of God's most powerful storm systems.

# THUNDER COUNT

*He fills his hands with lightning*
*and commands it to strike its mark.*
*His thunder announces the coming storm;*
*even the cattle make known its approach.*
*Job 36:32-33*

**The** windows rattle, the house shakes, and your dog hides under the bed. No, it's not a runaway freight train, it's just a thunderstorm. The sound of thunder frightens many people because of the loud noise, but in reality it is just a natural part of God's water cycle.

The loud bang of thunder is produced as a result of the energy of lightning. When lightning strikes, it heats up the air. This hot air expands very quickly then cools off and contracts. When these molecules of air are moving back and forth, it produces the sound waves that we hear as thunder.

Thunder always follows lightning because it takes the heat and energy of the lightning to produce the sound waves. You can learn to tell how far away a lightning strike is from the sound of thunder.

Observe a thunderstorm from your window and watch for lightning. As soon as you see a bolt of lightning flash across the sky, start timing and listening for the sound of thunder. When you hear the thunder, write down the number of seconds. Every five seconds equals 1.2 miles. So if it is five seconds from the lightning strike until you hear the thunder, the lightning is only 1.2 miles away.

The reason you don't hear the thunder immediately when you see the lightning is because light travels faster than the speed of sound. The light you see travels at the amazing speed of 186,000 miles per second. Sound travels at a much slower 1,100 feet per second.

As you listen to the thunderstorm, check your time. If the time between lightning and thunder is decreasing, the storm is moving toward you. If the time is increasing, the storm is moving away.

# LIGHTNING SPARKS

*"Listen to this, Job;*
*stop and consider God's wonders.*
*Do you know how God controls the clouds and*
*makes his lightning flash?"*
Job 37:14-15

**Lightning** sizzling through the sky is an awesome reminder of the power of God's nature. The average lightning stroke is six miles long and can reach temperatures of 50,000 degrees Fahrenheit. Lightning can burn trees and cause prairie and forest fires.

But while lightning carries the potential for great destructive force, it is also a normal part of God's world. When God created the world, He used tiny building blocks called atoms. Everything is made up of atoms, and every atom has positive and negative electron charges. Most of the time the electron charges stay equal or neutral, but friction, one thing rubbing against another, can cause an object to gain or lose electron charges. This gain or loss of electrons results in static electricity, and sometimes static electricity results in a small spark or shock.

A simple example of static electricity can be seen when socks rub against carpeting. The friction between the socks and carpeting causes the loss of electron charges. Touching a light switch or television returns the charges and causes an electric spark.

This is exactly what happens with lightning. Lightning is created through the friction of clouds. The lighting that flashes across the sky is actually a giant static spark.

You can create a lightning storm in your bed and in your mouth with static electricity.

# LIGHTNING IN YOUR MOUTH

After you darken the room, wait a few seconds for your eyes to adjust to the light, then put two of the Life Savers in your mouth and chew in front of the mirror. This is the one time you have permission to chew with your mouth open.

The friction of your teeth breaking the sugar crystals causes electric sparks. The wintergreen oil in the candy makes it easier for you to see the electricity. This lightning storm has a lot less power than those in nature, but it works with the same force of static electricity.

What You Need:

- Dark room
- One package of wintergreen Life Savers candy
- Mirror

# LIGHTNING IN YOUR BED

**What You Need:**

- Wool or synthetic blanket
- Your own hair

This experiment works best at night when you can make your room completely dark. Simply turn out the lights and jump under the covers. Rub the blanket on your hair. Remember this rubbing action causes friction. After a few seconds, pull the blanket away from your hair. You will see bright sparks of electricity moving back and forth from your hair to the blanket.

# THE RAINBOW'S BEGINNING

*"I have set my
rainbow in the
clouds,
and it will be the
sign of
the covenant
between me
and the earth."
Genesis 9:13*

**The** rainbow arching through the sky must have been a beautiful sight to Noah and his family. Amazingly, God forgave the earth for its sins and promised to never flood the world again. As a sign of His covenant, God took the same rain that caused the flood, mixed it with sunshine, and created a rainbow, a sign of God's unending love.

You can make your own miniature rainbow and remember God's promise.

A rainbow is made when drops of water refract sunlight. This means the

- Baking pan full of clean water
- Small mirror
- One piece of white posterboard
- A sunny day

sun shines into the water and is broken down into the basic colors of light. These colors are red, orange, yellow, green, blue, and violet. Together these colors form white light, but separately, they make a rainbow.

Place the posterboard upright on the ground. You may need to lean it against a chair or a building. Place the pan of water in front of the posterboard. Hold the mirror facing the posterboard, opposite the pan of water and gently move the mirror until the sunlight strikes it. Watch the posterboard as you move the mirror. Hold the mirror still when you see a rainbow of color.

*Note: Be careful that you do not reflect the sunlight into your own or someone else's eyes. The bright sun can cause permanent damage to your eyes.*

# FROST FREEZE

*He has made everything beautiful in its time.*
*Ecclesiastes 3:11*

**How** can a drop of water be beautiful? It's useful for drinking and washing, but is it really beautiful? God can make even an ordinary drop of water into a beautiful work of art.

Frost is just a collection of tiny drops of frozen water, but it can form in beautiful patterns. That is because the frozen ice crystals grow together in geometric shapes.

Frost forms when the temperature of the ground is below freezing (32 degrees Fahrenheit, 0 degrees Celsius). The air that touches the ground cools, and the water vapor freezes into ice crystals. These ice crystals are

What You Need:

- Drinking glass
- Petroleum jelly
- Crushed ice
- ½ cup salt
- Dishtowel

called frost. Frost is more likely to form on cold, clear nights because the temperature of the ground drops faster when there's no cloud cover for heat insulation.

Because frost crystals are clear and reflect the light, frost can be a dazzling display of God's weather. You can watch frost crystals grow in your own kitchen.

Use a clean, dry drinking glass that is room temperature. Dip your finger in the petroleum jelly and carefully write your first initial on the front of the glass. Set the glass on the dishtowel and fill the glass to the rim with crushed ice. Pour the ½ cup of salt over the ice. Watch the glass, and in a few minutes you will see frost form on the outside of the glass.

Frost will not form on your initial because the water crystals cannot cling to the petroleum jelly. Try the experiment again and make a new design with the petroleum jelly. You can use God's frost to make water look beautiful!

1/2 Cup

# TEMPERATURE TEST

*He performs wonders that cannot be fathomed,*
*miracles that cannot be counted.*
*He bestows rain on the earth;*
*he sends water upon the countryside.*
Job 5:9-10

**God** has richly blessed the earth with its changing weather patterns. There is rain to make plants grow on the land and snow to cover the mountaintops. One of the ways God creates weather is through the changes in temperature on the surface of the earth.

The rays of the sun are more intense around the middle of the earth, so the equator regions of the earth are constantly warm. The sun's rays are less intense at the poles, so the North Pole and South Pole of the earth are constantly cold. These vast differences in temperature combined with the slant of the earth make the seasons.

In most parts of the world, seasons are marked by some sort of temperature change. Temperature changes can also indicate coming storms or fair weather. Reading

**What You Need:**
- Empty 2-liter clear plastic pop bottle without lid
- Modeling clay
- Long drinking straw
- Water
- Food coloring
- Ruler
- Refrigerator
- Hot summer day

temperature changes is one of the basic tools of weather prediction.

A thermometer is the tool people use to record the temperature. The Italian mathematician (an expert in mathematics) Galileo invented the first scientific thermometer around 1600. Thermometers work because molecules expand when they are hot and contract when they are cold. As the liquid in the thermometer gets warm, it rises up the tube of the thermometer. As the liquid gets cold, the molecules contract and the liquid goes down in the tube.

You can make your own simple thermometer to check the changes in temperature.

Fill the bottom of the pop bottle with 1 inch of water. Make sure the water is room temperature. Add two drops of food coloring and mix the water and food coloring together.

Place the bottle on a level surface and stand the straw straight up in the bottle. Use the clay to seal the top of the bottle so that no air can get in. Do NOT put any clay over the top of the straw.

Look at your thermometer and note where the water is in the straw.

Carefully transport your thermometer outside to a sunny area. Let it sit for ten minutes and watch what happens to the water in the straw. It rises because the temperature outside is warmer than inside.

Now put your thermometer in the refrigerator. What do you suppose will happen to the water in the straw?

# HOMEGROWN HAIL

*Then the LORD said to Moses, "Stretch out your hand toward the sky so that hail will fall all over Egypt—on men and animals and on everything growing in the fields of Egypt."*

*Exodus 9:22-24*

**God** used the destructive force of hail to help free the Israelites from Egypt by creating the worst storm the Egyptians had ever seen.

Hail is actually a layered pellet of ice that forms during a thunderstorm. It is the only form of frozen precipitation that falls during warm weather. During a thunderstorm, rain is stored in the upper cloud layers as tiny ice crystals. Normally these ice crystals attract water droplets to form raindrops and melt as they fall to Earth. But in some thunderstorms, the air currents push the melting ice crystals back up to the top layers of the clouds where they freeze again. These crystals keep bouncing up and down, gathering layers of ice each time they move until they become so heavy that gravity pulls them to the ground.

Amazingly, some hail can keep bouncing in the clouds so long that they become very large. The record for the largest hailstone is held by Coffeyville, Kansas, where a hailstone weighing 1.67 pounds (0.75 kilograms) was found in 1970. In 1936, a hailstorm in South Africa dumped 3 feet of hail on the ground. An even more amazing fact is that in 1882, two frogs were found inside a hailstone in Dubuque, Iowa.

If you were to cut open a piece of hail, you would see that it has layers like an onion. A new layer of frozen water is created each time the hailstone bounces up and down in the clouds.

You can create your own hail with water and a freezer.

What You Need:

- *An assistant*
  - *Water*
- *Eyedropper*
- *Cookie sheet*
  - *Freezer*
- *Wax paper*
- *Magnifying glass*

Your hailstones will not be perfectly round with this experiment, but remember that hailstones come in all different sizes and shapes. Most hail is spherical (round), but hail can also form into the shape of stars, cones, and discs.

Place the wax paper on the cookie sheet. Use your eyedropper to carefully place ten drops of water on the cookie sheet.

Remember to keep the cookie sheet level at all times so the drops of water will not run together.

Have your assistant open the freezer door and place the cookie sheet inside. Make sure it is level in the freezer. Remove the cookie sheet from the freezer after twenty or thirty minutes. Place another drop of water on each small piece of ice. Replace it in the freezer. You will need to repeat this step at least six times, but you may do it more if you want to. Remember the more layers of water you add, the larger your hailstones.

After you have grown your hailstones to the size you want, remove them from the wax paper and look at them under a magnifying glass. You should be able to see a layer of ice for each layer of water you added to your hailstone.

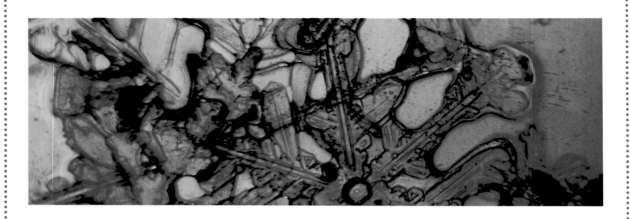

# SNOWFLAKES FOREVER

*Wash me, and I will be whiter than snow.*

*Psalm 51:7*

**When** snow cloaks the ground, it looks as though God gently covered the earth with a beautiful, pure white blanket. But if you look closely, you will find the blanket is made from millions of individual snowflakes, and no two snowflakes will be the same. Snow is just one more example of the infinite beauty and variety of God's work.

Snow forms only under certain conditions. Clouds must have enough liquid to form precipitation and, at the same time, the air temperature must be 32 degrees Fahrenheit (0 degrees Celsius) or lower. Because the air temperature is at the freezing point for water, the precipitation crystallizes and falls in the form of snow instead of rain.

The shape of the snowflake depends on the way the water molecules join together when they freeze. There are seven basic patterns for snowflakes, and each one of the flakes within a pattern forms a little differently. That is why no two snowflakes are ever the same. The basic shapes are shown on page 72.

# SNOWFLAKE CHART

Spatial Dendrite

Column

Stellar

Plate

Needle

Capped Column

Irregular Crystal

To truly appreciate the intricate variety of God's snowflakes, try to catch some and preserve them.

You will need to assemble these supplies well in advance of the first snowfall. Place the clean glass, the tweezers, and lacquer spray in the freezer to cool for at least 24 hours.

When it begins to snow, use the tweezers to take the glass plate out of the freezer. (Make sure you do not touch the glass with your hands or it will warm up the glass and melt the snowflakes.)

Take the glass plate and lacquer spray outside. Spray one side of the glass evenly with lacquer. Lay the glass on the ground and wait for a snowflake to land on it.

After you "catch" a snowflake on the glass plate, move it to a sheltered spot where no more snow can land on it. Leave the glass outside for two hours.

When you bring the glass inside, you can use the magnifying glass to view the print of your snowflake. This snowflake print can last for years and remind you of the beautiful variety of God's creation.

# ICE POWER

*The breath of God produces ice,*
*and the broad waters become frozen.*

*Job 37:10*

We skate on it, play on it, put it in our drinks, and even use it to reduce swelling of our injuries. Ice is such a part of our everyday life that sometimes we take it for granted. As humans we have so many uses for ice that sometimes we forget God uses ice as one of his tools for changing the face of the earth.

Most substances shrink as they get colder but water starts to expand when it reaches about 39 degrees Fahrenheit (4 degrees Celsius). The increase in size is what causes water pipes to burst in the winter. It also causes rocks and boulders to crack. During warm weather, water settles in small crevices in the rocks. When the water turns to ice, it expands and starts to break apart the rock. The ice changes large boulders into small stones and breaks stones into gravel.

You can witness the expansion and contraction of ice by freezing a coffee can full of water.

Fill the coffee can to the very top with water. Snap the lid into place. Put one ruler under the bottom of the can. Be sure to keep the can balanced so it does not tip. Place the small spool on top of the lid with the flat side down. The spool should not roll. Put the other ruler on top of the spool. Wind the tape around the ends of each ruler. This will form tape bands on each side of the can and will hold the rulers in place.

Carefully place the experiment in the freezer and leave it untouched for 24 hours. When the water is frozen you should see that the ice has pushed up the lid and the ruler has cracked. This is how God uses ice to break rocks and change the mountains.

What You Need:

- **Metal can with plastic snap lid** (a small coffee can or a peanut can)
- **Small spool**
- **Two old rulers or thin slats of wood (12 inches)**
- **Clear tape**
- **Water**
- **Freezer**

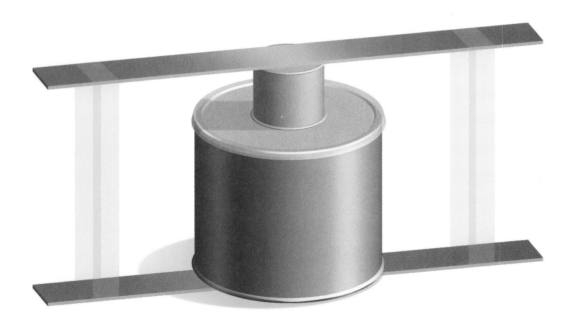

# EYE OF THE STORM

*He stilled the storm to a whisper;*
*the waves of the sea were hushed.*
*Psalm 107:29*

**Violent** storms can be frightening and even dangerous. The power of God's weather is not something to be taken for granted. In biblical times, people could only watch the sky to learn of the coming weather. Fishermen were often caught out at sea during violent storms and many lost their lives.

Today scientists monitor weather conditions on the ground through a network of more than 10,000 weather stations around the world. Buoys and

weather ships gather information about the weather conditions over the earth's oceans, and radar and satellites collect information on changing air conditions.

Scientists are able to give hourly updates of the changing weather, and people benefit from the forecasting by knowing whether the weather will be safe for outdoor activities.

You can keep up with the God's ever changing weather and learn more about how weather systems work by exploring the Internet.

If you do not have the Internet in your home, you may be able to use the Internet at your local library or public school.

# CHECK OUT THESE WEB SITES

The Weather Channel Home Page ................................... www.weather.com

Owlie Skywarning ...................................................... www.crh.noaa.gov

USA Today Weather ................................................... www.usatoday.com

Federal Emergency Management Association

.............................................................................. www.fema.gov/kids/

The Weather Dude by forecaster Nick Walker ............. www.wxdude.com

Everything you wanted to know about weather ........ www.tvweather.com

Dan's Wild Weather Page .................................. www.whnt19.com/kidwx

Missouri Botanical Garden's

   Climate and Ecosystems .................................. www.mbgnet.mobot.org

Kids' Web Weather ..www.npac.syr.edu/textboo/schoolweb/weather.html

National Severe Storms Laboratory ........................... www.nssl.noaa.gov

# BIBLIOGRAPHY

Ardley, Neil. *The Science Book Of Weather.* London: Dorling Kindersly, 1992.

Christian, Spencer. *Can It Really Rain Frogs?* New York: John Wiley and Sons, 1997.

Cosgrove, Brian. *Eyewitness Books Weather.* New York: Alfred A. Knopf, 1991.

Elsom, Derek. *Weather Explained.* New York: Henry Holt and Company, 1997.

Haslam, Andrew. *Make It Work!* United Kingdom: Weather, World Book Publishing, 1997.

Lafferty, Peter. *Science Facts Weather.* New York: Crescent Books, 1992.

Mandell, Muriel. *Simple Weather Experiments.* New York: Sterling Publishing Company, 1990.

McVey, Viki. *Weather Wisdom.* San Francisco: Sierra Books, 1991.

Peacock, Graham. *Meteorology.* New York: Thomas Learning, 1995.

VanCleave, Janice. *Weather.* New York: John Wiley and Sons, 1995.

**Meet Stephanie Finke:** I am an educator with over seventeen years of experience. Over those years, I have been privileged to teach in a variety of settings including public, private, and parochial schools. I also served as the director of children's education at Missouri Botanical Garden.

My experience with children has led me to realize that many people, even Christians, tend to view science as separate and apart from God. Growing up with a biology teacher as a father, I was always taught that science is just a tool we use to learn more about God's creation. Without God, there would be no science.

Currently, I am a second grade teacher at Benton Elementary School in St. Charles, Missouri where I try to instill a sense of wonder and a quest for knowledge in my students. At home, I use my two children, Nichole and Joshua, as guinea pigs for my experiments. They have become experts at exploding rockets and cleaning up lava spills. My husband Alan has learned to ignore the strange things that grow in our refrigerator and nobody has eaten one of my experiments. . .yet!